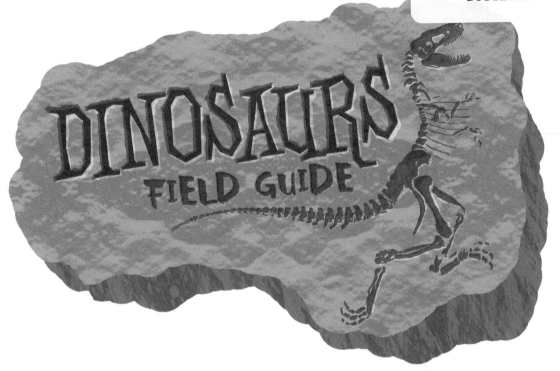

DINOSAURS FIELD GUIDE

DOVER

Dover Publications, Inc.
Mineola, New York

Copyright

Copyright © 2013 by Dover Publications, Inc.
All rights reserved.

Bibliographical Note

Dinosaurs Field Guide, first published by Dover Publications, Inc., in 2013,
is a new compilation of both new and revised published material.

International Standard Book Number

ISBN-13: 978-0-486-49156-1
ISBN-10: 0-486-49156-0

Manufactured in the United States by LSC Communications
49156005   2019
www.doverpublications.com

Layout and Design by Hourglass Press

Dinosaurs

With the prevalence of dinosaur references in our modern culture, it's easy to think of them as very matter of fact, without thinking too much about the reality of their existence and their relation to modern life. It's important not to forget how amazing it is that we even know about animals that lived millions of years ago, let alone know the details that we do. It's important, though, to realize how little material paleontologists actually have to work with. Many species of dinosaur are known from a single, likely incomplete, fossil. Our understanding of these creatures and the very different world they inhabited is ever changing as more information is made available and new theories are developed.

The "age of reptiles," known as the Mesozoic era, occurred approximately 240 million years ago to 65 million years ago (by comparison, humans have been on Earth for less than 1 million years). This era consisted of three periods—the Triassic, Jurassic, and Cretaceous—each of which had different global conditions and collections of life.

When the Mesozoic era began, all of the continents were connected into one "supercontinent," Pangaea. During the Triassic period, weather was consistently hot and dry and there were no polar ice caps, so water levels were higher. Small early dinosaurs appeared during this period, which lasted about 40 million years, before a massive extinction event wiped out most dinosaurs.

Next was the Jurassic period, which lasted from about 208 million years ago to 145 million years ago. Pangaea started to break apart during this period and the Earth began to develop different climates. More dinosaurs evolved at this time, including the giant ones we think of today. Early dinosaur-like birds also began to develop at this time.

The Cretaceous period, spanning from around 145 million years ago to 65 million years ago, was when dinosaurs really flourished. The broken-apart Pangaea started to look like the continental geography we know today and temperatures significantly dropped at the North and South poles. It was during this period that the majority of dinosaurs coexisted.

The Mesozoic era ended with the K-T mass extinction, 65 million years ago, which wiped out the last of the remaining dinosaur species.

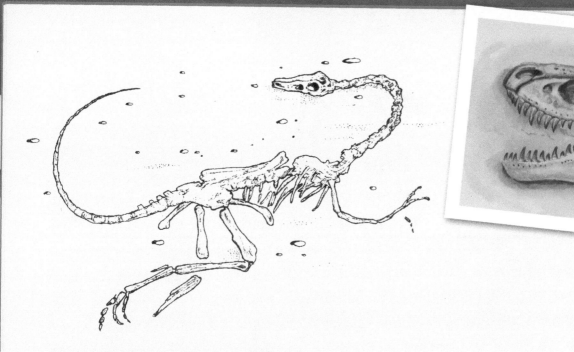

LEAVING BEHIND SOME CLUES

Our knowledge of dinosaurs comes entirely from the discovery and study of fossils. Archaeologists usually have to dig up areas in search of the fossils, while being careful not to damage any part of the fossils. Occasionally, though, fossils are discovered right on the surface in plain view. Dinosaur fossils have been discovered on all seven continents, and it's possible to find them almost anywhere.

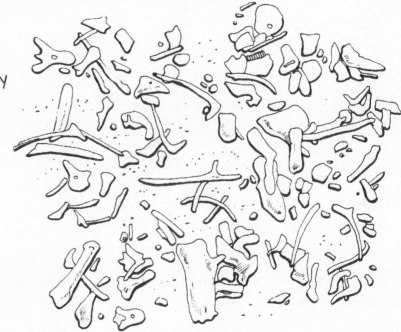

The most informative fossils we've found have been in the form of skeletons, but fossils have also been discovered for nests, eggs, and footprints. A common misconception is that fossils are actually dinosaur skeletons, when in fact they are more similar to rocks, which over time have merged with and taken the place of the original skeletons.

A lot can be determined from a fossil. For example, a skull alone can tell you whether a dinosaur was a carnivore or herbivore, how big its brain was, or whether it had good eyesight.

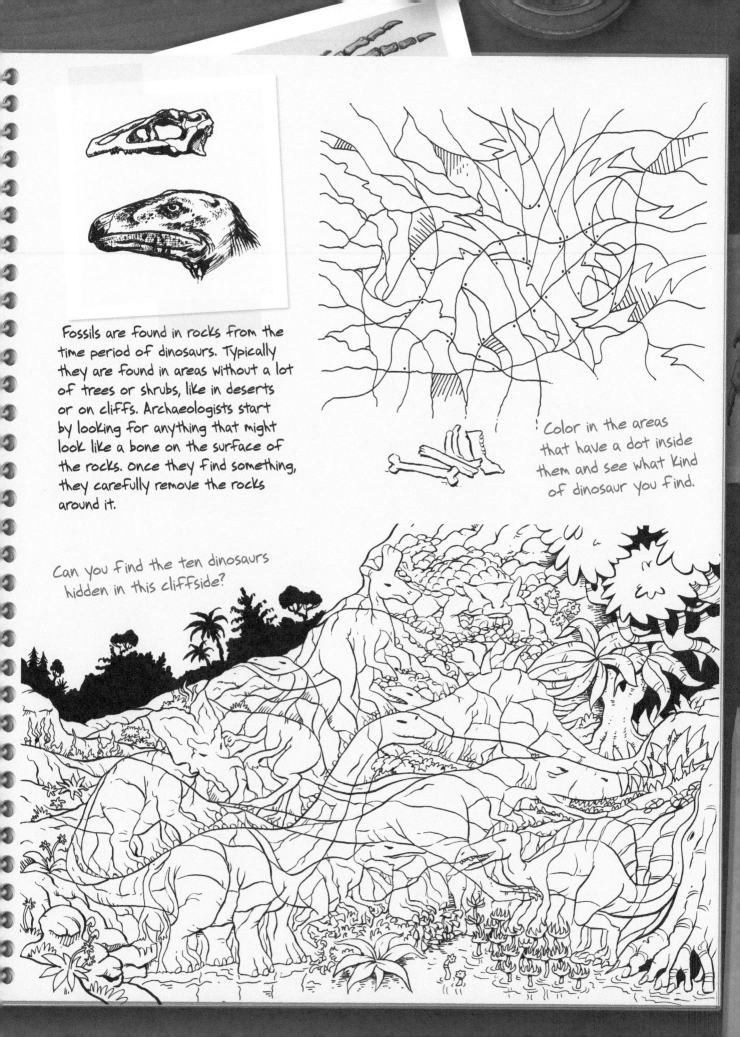

Fossils are found in rocks from the time period of dinosaurs. Typically they are found in areas without a lot of trees or shrubs, like in deserts or on cliffs. Archaeologists start by looking for anything that might look like a bone on the surface of the rocks. once they find something, they carefully remove the rocks around it.

Can you find the ten dinosaurs hidden in this cliffside?

Color in the areas that have a dot inside them and see what Kind of dinosaur you find.

Find your way to the dinosaur fossil.

Velociraptors

Velociraptors were pack-hunting predators measuring about 6 ½ feet in length. One of the defining features of this dinosaur is its large, curved claw, which it used to attack and rip open its prey. Studies show that velociraptors are closely related to modern-day birds of prey like hawks and eagles, which have a similar hook claw.

able to discern that the dilophosaurus ate
based on the remains found either within
ich is thought to b

Dilophosaurus

The dilophosaurus was a bipedal carnivore from the early part of the Jurassic period. It lived nearly 200 million years ago and was one of the earliest known carnivorous dinosaurs. Its name means double-crested lizard, in reference to the two ridges on the top of its head.

Based on the formation of their teeth and jaws, the dilophosaurs were likely scavengers. The space between their teeth indicates that these dinosaurs probably weren't strong enough to hold down and kill another dinosaur, leading paleontologists to believe they ate dead or dying dinosaurs.

Fig. 9
The frills on the Dilophosaurus's head, for which it is named.

DILOPHOSAURUS

Triceratops

The name "triceratops" literally means "three-horned face," which is the defining feature of this Cretaceous-period dinosaur. In addition to horns, the triceratops also had a large plate, or a "frill," on the back of its head. Paleontologists believe that the frill may have helped the triceratops to cool off, or it may have been for display.

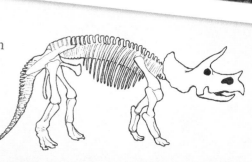

Fig. 3
Triceratops skeleton

The T. rex had 50 to 60 blade-like teeth, some up to 12 inches long!

When one broke or fell out, a new one would grow in its place, creating a cluster of jagged teeth.

Fig. 13
Tyrannosaurus rex foot measuring abou[t]
3.3 feet long

Tyrannosaurus rex

Possibly the most famous of the dinosaurs, the Tyrannosaurus rex (meaning "tyrant lizard king"), or T. rex for short, was a fierce bipedal predator. Standing at 20 feet tall and measuring nearly 40 feet long, the T. rex still wasn't the biggest carnivore to walk the earth, but with its good vision, strong arms and legs, fast speed, and jaws capable of crushing bones, it was hard to match its power.

The T. rex's head is large and wide with many openings in the skull for strong jaw muscles and a narrow snout to allow for better vision. Its jaws are more than 4 feet long. Its tail, at more than 15 feet long, was used to help balance its large head and heavy torso, keeping it from tipping over and helping it turn when running. With a 15-foot stride, the Tyrannosaurus rex is believed to have run at speeds up to 20 miles per hour!

Euoplocephalus

The euoplocephalus was one of many types of armored dinosaurs.
It had a club on the end of its tail and spikes along its body.

The ceratosaurus was about 20 feet long, but half of that was its lengthy tail.

This dinosaur had a horn on its nose that is believed to have been primarily for display.

The tuojiangosaurus is similar to the more widely known stegosaurus, but had spikes along its back instead of flat plates.

Nobody knows for certain what color it was.

B A W N C T S S E W Y H K M O B P I
X L N P I D A T W L V P U R T L T Q
A B V W T A I E I U E Q P L R A E E
P E K E R F G S I F R A E A I I R A
A R F O L S S D C H C O P Y C R O X
D T T L P O W A E U A E K P E D S O
I O P U F A C V I X E R M T R U A G
P S Y R T Y C I T I P A T I A E U K
L A N A I A F A R E G I W R T A R I
O U Z V O P Z W S A U R O P O D S J
D R W P H A S P J E P S T S P X L G
O U T F O E S U F A I T Q A S R G U
C S C O N C H O R A P T O R L E P O
U E X U R S A U R O P T E R Y G I A
S P I W D I P F O Q O C U

Can you find the words on this list in the jumble of letters above?

VELOCIRAPTOR
PTEROSAURS
TRICERATOPS
SAUROPODS
CONCHORAPTOR
CITIPATI
DIPLODOCUS
FOSSIL
EGG
SAUROPTERYGIA
ALBERTOSAURUS

13

Tyrannosaurids have been found on all three northern continents.

So far, triceratops and pachycephalosaurus fossils have been found exclusively in western North America.

Interestingly, similar species of dilophosaurus have been found in both North America and China.

The amargasaurus was found in central Argentina.

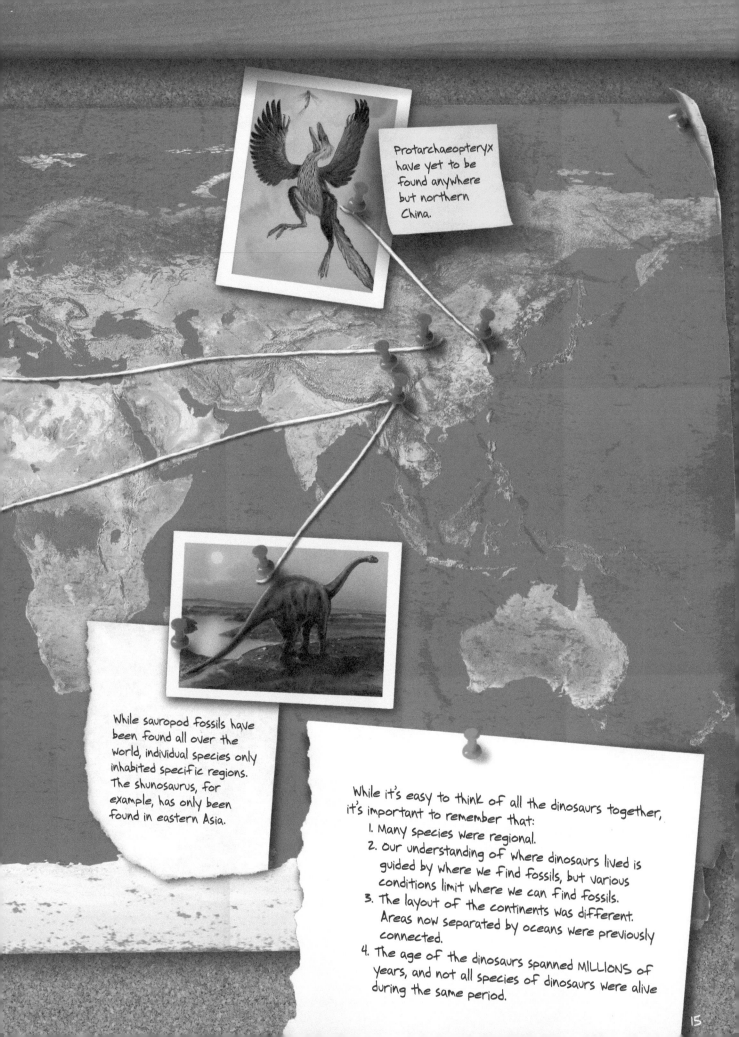

Protarchaeopteryx have yet to be found anywhere but northern China.

While sauropod fossils have been found all over the world, individual species only inhabited specific regions. The shunosaurus, for example, has only been found in eastern Asia.

While it's easy to think of all the dinosaurs together, it's important to remember that:
1. Many species were regional.
2. Our understanding of where dinosaurs lived is guided by where we find fossils, but various conditions limit where we can find fossils.
3. The layout of the continents was different. Areas now separated by oceans were previously connected.
4. The age of the dinosaurs spanned MILLIONS of years, and not all species of dinosaurs were alive during the same period.

ALBERTOSAURUS

The Albertosaurus is a tyrannosaurid, and an ancestor to the more widely known Tyrannosaurus rex. Growing to about 30 feet in length and weighing nearly 2 tons, Albertosaurus is still one of the smallest in the tyrannosaurid family. It gets its name from the place its fossils have been found, in Alberta, Canada.

Albertosaurus fossils have been found in groups, leading paleontologists to believe they traveled in herds or packs. With predatorial features similar to the T. rex, these dinosaurs would have been extremely threatening in numbers.

Tyrannosaurids are often pictured attacking other large dinosaurs, but they would also regularly eat smaller animals.

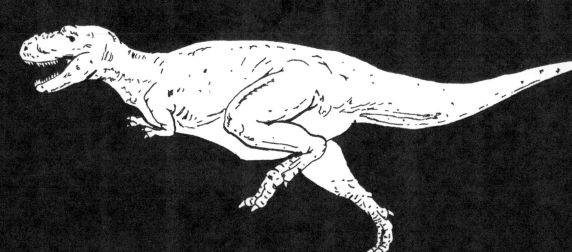

Hold this page up to
the light to reveal the
albertosaurus skeleton.

Archaeologists have to estimate
what a dinosaur's body looked like
based on its skeletal structure.
The exact bone order and posture
of dinosaurs will always be in question.
A lot of features aren't necessarily
revealed by a skeleton. That's why
you'll see the same dinosaur depicted
different ways.

Like many dinosaurs, tyrannosaurids' eyes were located on the sides of their head. This leads scientists to believe that they had poor vision.

Most dinosaurs had long tails to help balance their large heads and torsos.

Tyrannosaurids had short arms with only 2 digits.

The Albertosaurus, like other tyrannosaurids, was bipedal, which means that it only walked on its hind legs.

The ankle joint was part of the leg, which lengthened its stride. Albertosaurus are believed to have walked about 10 to 12 miles per hour and to have run up to 25-30 miles per hour.

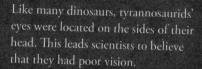

ALBERTOSAURUS SKELETON

Large openings in tyrannosaurids' skulls reduced the weight and left more space for muscle.

An Albertosaurus's head measured as much as 3 ½ feet long.

Even though it was one of the smaller tyrannosaurids, the Albertosaurus had up to 58 teeth, which is more than larger species of the family.

Spot the difference

Find the one complete skeleton, and draw an arrow to the missing piece in the others.

It's extremely difficult to collect every single one of the bones in a dinosaur, as they're easily lost over time. Museums will make replicas of missing pieces to fill holes and complete a skeleton.

Fig. 1
Anchiceratops

Fig. 2
Styracosaurus

Fig. 3
Pachyrhinosaurus

Fig. 4
Centrosaurus

Fig. 5
Chasmosaurus

Fig. 6
Saurolophus

Fig. 7
Pachycephalosaurus

Fig. 8
Homalocephale

Fig. 9
Parasaurolophus

Fig. 11
Tyrannosaurus Rex

Fig. 12
Herrerasaurus

A lot of dinosaur species have very distinctive skulls that make them easy to identify. Notice the varying characteristics visible in the species shown above. Figures 1-5 are all Ceratopsians, with beaks and a neck-covering frill. Other features include thickened armor, small spikes, and crests.

Corythosaurus

Lambeosaurus

Parasaurolophus

Iguanodon

Malasaurus

Tenontosaurus

BONE HEADS

Can you tell which skull goes with which dinosaur? Draw lines to match them by shape.

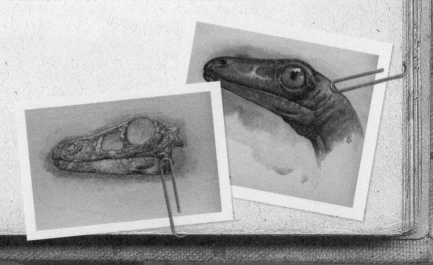

The function of the plates on the stegosaurus's back is not known for certain. Some scientists theorize that the plates were for protection against predators, while others say they helped control body temperature.

Stegosauruses have 4 long spikes at the very end of their tails, which were are about 2-3 feet long. They protruded horizontally and were most likely used in combat against attackers.

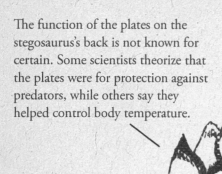

The stegosaurus had an unusual posture, with a tail that appears to be about 6 feet off the ground.

The small head of the stegosaurus only had enough space inside the skull for a brain about the size of a walnut.

Some scientists theorize that stegosauruses were able to stand on their longer, sturdier hind legs to reach food in higher places.

Stegosaurus

The stegosaurus is the largest of the stegosaurid genus. It lived during the later part of the Jurassic period, around 155 to 150 million years ago. This large herbivore is very easily identified by the diamond-shaped plates down its back and tail. This dinosaur measured up to 30 feet long and more than 12 feet tall. Though it had a large body, its head was disproportionately small and had very small, flat teeth.

The stegosaurus's odd posture positioned its head close to the ground, most likely for grazing and foraging for shrubs and other low-lying foods. Its small, flat teeth would have been used for pulling and tearing food, but not grinding. From this, scientists can determine that its diet most likely consisted of softer, smaller plants such as mosses and ferns. It is also likely that it would have swallowed small stones to help grind up the food inside its stomach.

The rocks a stegosaurus would swallow to help grind its food are known as gastroliths.

As with other dinosaurs, the tail's length in relation to the body increased the lesothosaurus's balance and its ability to move quickly.

Large cavities in the skull accommodated large eyes and strong facial muscles for shredding and chewing.

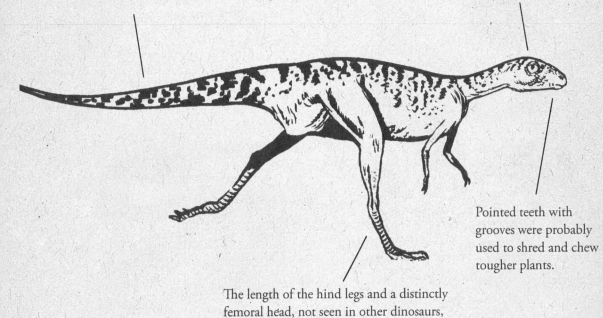

Pointed teeth with grooves were probably used to shred and chew tougher plants.

The length of the hind legs and a distinctly femoral head, not seen in other dinosaurs, suggest that the lesothosaurus was a fast, agile runner.

Lesothosaurus

The lesothosaurus was one of the smallest dinosaurs that ever lived. With its short neck, it likely looked like a large modern-day lizard, but standing on long hind legs.

The lesothosaurus was about 3 ½ feet long and 18 inches tall, about the height of a chicken.

Very little has been established about the species due to the rarity of its fossils.

Though it had sharp, pointed teeth, they fit together in a way that leads paleontologists to believe these dinosaurs were herbivores. They had hollow bones, like birds, which would have made them very light and fast, and helped them to evade predators.

DINO ARMOR

In order to protect themselves from fierce predators like the T. rex, a number of dinosaur species developed defensive armor.

One group of dinosaurs, ankylosaurs, developed a distinct body armor. These gentle herbivores generally had short legs and small brains, making them slow and unintelligent. An easy target like the ankylosaur had to have some kind of defense. Some had spikes running the lengths of their backs and tails, and some had big clubs at the ends of their tails. These clubs are called thagomizers, and sometimes featured spikes up to 3 feet long. Their armor usually covered all but their underbelly. Though ankylosaurs were slow and therefore vulnerable, their protections meant it would have taken quite a bit of effort to kill these sturdy dinosaurs. Their low stance gave them great balance to stand their ground while they swung their mighty tails into the attacking predator.

Thagomizers

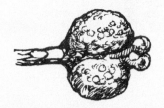

Pachycephalosaurus

The pachycephalosauria were a group of medium-sized dinosaurs from the late Cretaceous period. Pachycephalosaurus literally means thick-headed lizard, which refers to the large dome on the tops of their heads. These domes were solid and usually several inches thick. Some were flat on top while others were more cone shaped, and often surrounded by a series of horns of varying lengths and sharpnesses.

These dinosaurs had long hind legs and short arms, making them bipedal. Pachycephalosaurus had a spine that was reinforced with a solid structure and strong muscles, which allowed these dinosaurs to make their bodies very straight when they looked down and pointed the tops of their head forward. They could essentially turn themselves into battering rams. Paleontologists speculate that this ramming behavior was used either for defense or to compete with other males for females' attention.

FOLLOW THE HERD Each parasaurolophus has a twin in the herd. Can you find each dinosaur's match?

GRID DRAWING Draw each of these squares in its corresponding space on the next page.

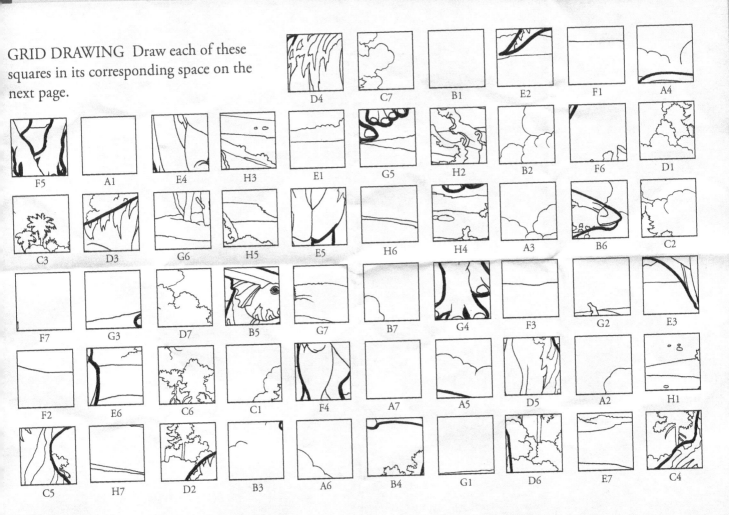

	1	2	3	4	5	6	7
A							
B							
C							
D							
E							
F							
G							
H							

Parasaurolophus

This herbivorous dinosaur was both bipedal and quadrupedal. It primarily moved around on all fours, and would stand up on its hind legs to forage for plants in higher places. Its duckbill has led some scientists to believe the Parasaurolophus was a land and water dweller—fossilized stomach contents mainly consisted of land plants such as pine needles, twigs, and leaves. One of the defining features of this dinosaur is the long backward-facing crest protruding from its head. The crest is hollow, consisting of 4 tubes that start at the parasaurolophus's nostrils, run all the way up the top of the head to the tip of the crest, and turn back under where they attach to the skull.

Height Chart

50 ft.
45 ft.
40 ft.
35 ft.
30 ft.
25 ft.
20 ft.
15 ft.
10 ft.
5 ft.

school bus

Ankylosaurus   Velociraptor   Adult human   Triceratops   Stegosaurus

SAFETY IN SIZE?

Luckily for some of the largest herbivores, not only did they severely outnumber the carnivores but, thanks to their size, they really only needed to worry about the largest and most aggressive of the carnivores. Any predator that was too small could easily be crushed or whipped away with their massive tails or feet. It would have been not only difficult but probably very intimidating to attack a herd of these large dinosaurs.

— 3-story house

Parasaurolophus   Tyrannosaurus rex   Brontosaurus

Sauropods

Sauropods are identified by their long necks, long tails, and small heads. They include the sauroposeidon, the tallest dinosaur (and the largest animal to ever walk on land!). Their fossils have been found on every continent, including Antarctica.

Sauropods' height and long necks enabled them to reach foliage outside the reach of most herbivores. Impressively, their massive hind legs were capable of supporting their weight, enabling them to reach even higher points. Standing upright would also have made them extremely intimidating to any other dinosaurs that may have preyed on them.

56 ft. tall!

Sauroposeidon – 112 ft. long

long neck made up half of overall length

Mamenchisaurus – 43 ft. long

(armored plates along back)

Saltasaurus – 39 ft. long

Amargasaurus – 33 ft. long

Feathers?

It's been known for some time that some dinosaurs had feathers, as is evident by fossils like this one, belonging to an archaeopteryx. But until recently, most dinosaurs had been depicted with rough, leathery skin much like a lizard's. However, recent studies show that many, if not most, dinosaurs had feathers. Feathers did not signify flight, however, but were most likely used for display and insulation from extreme weather conditions.

Dinosaurs we've been picturing one way for decades are now being reimagined as colorful, feathered animals, highlighting how little definite information we have about these creatures.

Avimimus

The name Avimimus literally means "bird mimic." It was named this because it was one of the first dinosaurs believed to have had feathers. It also has an identifiable beak, similar to that of a parrot.

It lived about 85 million to 75 million years ago, in the Cretaceous period, along with predators like the Velociraptor and the T. rex. Although the Avimimus is small compared with other dinosaurs, at only 3 feet long, it was an omnivore, eating small animals, insects, and plants.

Conchoraptor

Conchoraptor is translated as "conch thieves," and was named for its assumed diet of shellfish. Instead of teeth, this oviraptorid had a large beak, which is thought to have been for crushing the hard shells of conch and other shelled creatures whose fossilized remains were found in similar areas. However, it is also possible that this feature was used for another purpose, like cracking nuts or eggs.

The conchoraptor was at one time thought to be an adolescent version of another dinosaur, the oviraptor, and that it developed the oviraptor's distinct crest when reaching maturity. Through continued study, though, paleontologists found distinct differences in the arms and hands of fossils and have determined that the conchoraptor was in fact a separate species. This is yet another example of our continually changing understanding of dinosaurs.

Citipati

At approximately 9 feet long, the citipati was long known as the largest of the oviraptorids (until the discovery of the 26-foot-long gigantoraptor in 2007).
It's well known as a result of well-preserved skeletons. Fossilized citipati in brooding positions over eggs changed the previously held belief that oviraptors were preying on the eggs commonly found in proximity to their own fossilized remains. This birdlike behavior is also responsible for paleontologists' early associations of dinosaurs with birds.

Protoarchaeopteryx

This little dinosaur was about the size of a turkey. Although it had long feathers on its arms and tail, it is believed this dinosaur could not fly. However, scientists believe that these dinosaurs could use a limited gliding ability to assist them in jumping from branch to branch in trees.

Velociraptor

The velociraptor is a prime example of a dinosaur that's previously been pictured without feathers by scientists, but more recently has been shown with varying feather coverage.

Color this picture of a Velociraptor.

Pterosaurs

Pterosaurs were flying reptiles that were prevalent during the age of dinosaurs, but unlike the feathered dinosaurs that closely resembled birds, pterosaurs weren't actually dinosaurs. Scientists consider dinosaurs a branch of the bird family, but pterosaurs are more closely related to present-day reptiles.

These flying reptiles varied greatly in size and height; they ranged from a few inches to more than 40 feet! Their wings consisted of skin, muscle, and other tissues that stretched from their ankles to the tip of their elongated 4th finger. They had beaks ranging in length, and though most had several needlelike teeth, some show no evidence of teeth at all.

Fill the sky with pterosaurs.

Plesiosaurs

Plesiosaurs were large aquatic reptiles that inhabited the oceans during the age of dinosaurs. Like pterosaurs, they aren't considered dinosaurs, even though they look very similar.

There were many species of plesiosauria. In the early Jurassic period they divided into two different groups, the long-necked and small-headed plesiosaurs and the short-necked and large-headed pliosaurs. The plesiosaurs ranged in sizes from 10 feet to nearly 45 feet, with most of their length coming from their necks. Their bodies were small in comparison to the much larger pliosaurs, but because their necks were long, they were very flexible. The large-headed palsiosaurs grew to about 40 feet long.

The legendary Loch Ness Monster is believed by some to be a surviving plesiousaur.

START

FINISH

Help the ammonite at the top left sneak past the long-necked elasmosaurus to find the other ammonites.

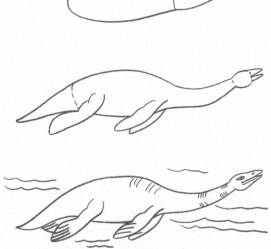

Draw an ocean full of plesiosaurs
and other prehistoric creatures.

A baby hadrosaurus emerging from its shell.

A hadrosaurus egg was about 10-11" long, just about the size and shape of a standard football.

Dino Eggs

Like modern reptiles, dinosaurs laid eggs. Unlike most modern reptiles, however, dinosaurs cared for and raised their young. Some dinosaurs, though, did lay eggs and leave them to hatch and survive on their own.

While many eggs have been found, they rarely have any type of fossilized remains inside to identify the dinosaur they're from.

Help the mother find all of the babies.

Maiasaura

The name Maiasaura means "caring mother lizard". These dinosaurs don't seem to have had defense mechanisms against predators, which is probably why they were herding dinosaurs, traveling and raising their young in large groups. Maiasaura nested close together, leaving no more than 20 feet between the nests, and usually laid about 30 to 40 eggs at a time.

Maiasaura

Dino Diet

Paleontologists can use the limited material available to them to make assumptions about what dinosaurs ate.

One of the biggest indicators of diet is the dinosaurs' teeth. Flat, blunt teeth indicate the species was an herbivore that used its teeth for pulling and grinding plants, while sharper teeth suggest the species was a carnivore, able to cut and tear away flesh with its jaws.

Fossilized stomach contents and dung have also been found. Interestingly, this has included rocks in some herbivores, which paleontologist believe were swallowed intentionally to help grind up tough, fibrous plants.

Smart creatures run and hide when they see an Allosaurus.

Can you find the 21 small mammals hiding in this picture?

Good Defense

In a world with so many threatening predators, dinosaurs had to be able to defend themselves. Ankylosaurs, like the edmontonia, euoplocephalus, and nodosaurus, had their armor; and stegosauria, like the tuojiangosaurus, wuerhosaurus, and kentrosaurus, had their spiked tails.

Ceratopsids are a group of species that have a large frill on the back of their heads. Many of the species also had horns on their faces. The horns made them dangerous when faced head on, while the frills protected the neck.

It's unknown how aggressive ceratopids were, but it's largely believed that a horned triceratops could cripple and mortally injure a T. rex by charging it.

Saurornithoides

These medium-sized carnivores were fast and strong. Sharp claws on their feet, and one especially long, sharp claw toe on each foot, would have been good for pinning down prey. They most likely preyed on small mammals and reptiles, chasing them down and catching them with their long arms.

Ornitholestes

This small carnivore's name means "bird robber," referring to its diet of small birds. These dinosaurs reached up to approximately 7 feet in length, but almost half of that was their long skinny tail, which gave them the balance and agility necessary to pursue their prey.

SOLUTIONS

Page 5

Page 5

Page 6

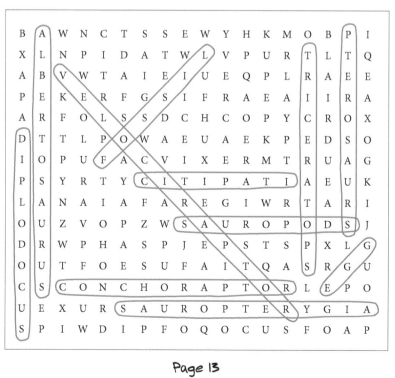

Page 13

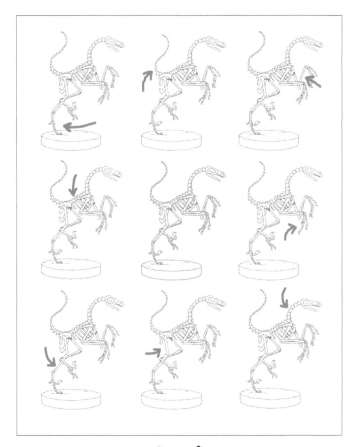

Page 19

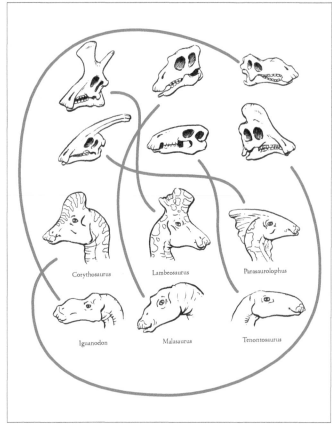

Page 21

Page 26

Page 27

Page 36

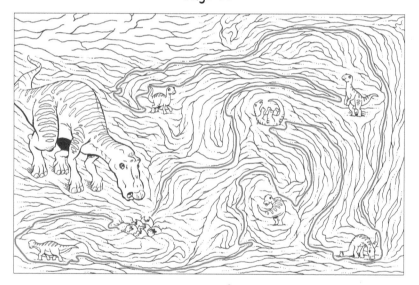

Page 39

Page 41